Praise for

How to Swim with the Sharks: A Survival Guide for Leadership in Diverse Environments
By Vickie L. McCray, MS, CISM, CGFM, CIO

"As a woman of color trying to prove myself in this global economy, this book gave me some great insights and ideas on how to navigate the tough world of work which is full of sharks. Often, those around the office are not straightforward and when you least expect it, attack you. But this book gave the support and made me realize that I am not alone in this battle."

-EFFIE BURWELL
Senior Musician,
Pleasant Green M.B. Church

How to Swim with the Sharks

A Survival Guide for Leadership in Diverse Environments

By Vickie L. McCray, MS, CISM, CGFM, CIO

How to Swim with the Sharks
Copyright © 2014 by Vickie L. McCray
All rights reserved.

No part of this publication may be reproduced, stored in a retrieval system or transmitted in any way by any means, electronic, mechanical, photocopy, recording or otherwise without written permission of the publisher except as provided by USA copyright law.

Author photo by: Patrick McCray

International Standard Book Number: 0692942262
Library of Congress Control Number: 2014944867

Published in the United States of America

"To Preston and June, my brothers, I think about you all the time."

Contents

Preface	*9*
Territory Battle	13
Temper Your Light or Lose It!	21
Dealing with Disappointments	35
Help, My Degree is Failing Me	43
Foggy Expectations	53
Loyalty Balance, a Juggling Act	61
Leaders Choose Diplomacy to Achieve Win-Win	69
Listening: Do You Hear What I Hear?	79
Your Worst Fears	87
Are You Ready for a Blessing?	93

Preface

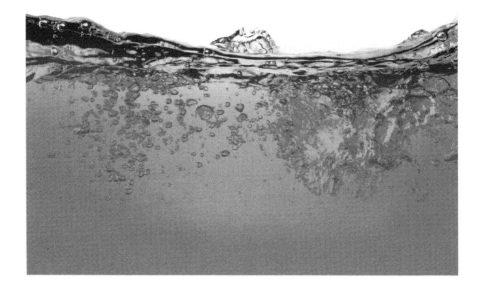

Throughout my career in both the public and private sectors, I have held leadership roles including team lead, audit manager, technical advisor, assistant executive director, project manager, and as program manager (my current role). A key requirement for maintaining the roles was always to attend management training. While these trainings had some useful information, the focus was on how to be a manager rather than how to be an effective leader.

Upon receiving my Master's in Information Studies from Syracuse University in New York, I was offered an opportunity to serve as an adjunct professor to teach leadership at graduate level. This is where it all began for me. This is where I saw firsthand the importance of leadership and of how politics was prevalent in every challenge. I learned so much during the teaching experience and discovered there are so many different leadership styles.

---------- ∽ ----------

I also realized that not everyone has the ability or the patience to be a leader, but everyone who wants to be a leader should at least try.

A few years later, I decided to write a book to tell the story about my career and include stories on leadership and politics. I've had an extensive career that has allowed me opportunities to excel. However, the leadership lessons were founded during the move toward senior management. As a leader, you have a choice—to lead or to follow. I chose to lead and with this decision, I chose to share a few of the lessons learned in my quest to become an effective leader.

One learns that it takes more than just wanting to be a good leader. You also have to exercise patience and diligence in doing the right thing to promote others more than yourself.

Leaders share information willingly and gain so much more when they care for their team. In the spirit of sharing, I chose to write about some of my experiences and of how I managed to work through the challenges to come out a winner. And in those instances where I was not always a winner, where it wasn't a win-win, well, this only means not now. It means that you should exercise patience and your time will come.

1
Territory Battle

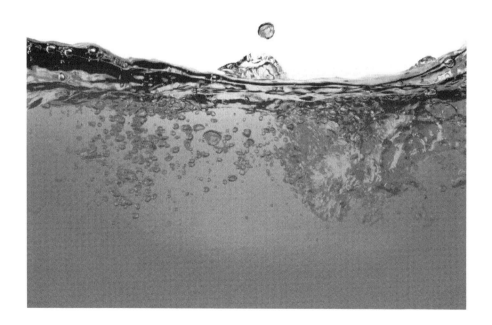

1
Territory Battle

Dilemma

Imagine two colleagues both with the same pedigree: college-educated, excellent communication skills, competent, hold a wealth of knowledge in their field of expertise, and described as good managers of both people and teams. The one drawback is both were selected to manage the same project. One can only imagine what transpired between the two highly educated, pontificating, drama queens. There was an immediate tug---of---war because one manager believed that her opinion was the gospel, while the other manager believed that he created the gospel. Interesting dichotomy. And when one manager disagreed with the other... you guessed it... diplomacy in the making. Yes, I am being facetious, but it is a start. Egos got in the way and sometimes clouded their judgments. It seems that one project manager always wanted to be the "bigger cheese" even though both were at the same level. The constant banter back and forth proves to be tiring and exhaustive. Finally, after all of the back and forth, one of the managers decides that enough is enough. That was the straw that broke the camel's back. One of the managers has to make a clear decision. As the song goes, "Should I stay or should I go?" It would be so easy to just say "I QUIT!" That's an easy out. But leaders do not quit. They come up with solutions to move the project along with a successful outcome. What would you do to move the project forward?

Strategy

This dilemma is real. I have witnessed it, and you probably have too. So, how do you tackle it? One of the managers or a higher---up will have to pause and evaluate this scenario objectively. One solution that has worked for me would be to recognize the strengths and weaknesses of each manager and to discuss how best to proceed with the project. In doing so, this action will create some sense of balance among the management styles. The result is that one of the managers takes on the role as a team member and without much pain, begins to listen attentively and provide suggestions when needed. These actions are quite humbling to the manager who takes on this role.

Advantage

While the other manager is barking orders, the manager who takes the team member role will be viewed as an effective manager. This leadership style commands and builds respect from colleagues because of one's willingness to listen and work collaboratively to bring the project to a successful end. This humble leader will be viewed as a *true* leader because he or she has decided, in a challenging situation, to swallow his/her pride. The focus, instead, is on the true goal—the success of the project. Humility is key and it really does work.

Reflection

Growing up, my grandma would often remind me of the importance of being humble. She used to say, "All you need is just a pinch of humility... it goes a long way." A pinch of humility is like the pinch of salt Grandma used in her infamous homemade pumpkin pies and scrumptious turkey and dressing. Too much salt was not good for the meal.

Just a pinch of humility should be applied in the office setting to manage a successful project. In peculiar situations, don't be afraid to step---down to get the job done. As a leader, you are placed in positions that may require patience while you are under attack. Grandma was right as a pinch of salt can make a stale meal taste so good!

Take-Aways

- Thoroughly evaluate the strengths and weaknesses of each manager as it relates to the project.
- Too many leaders is like putting in too much salt. For that reason, someone has to

step down.

- Knowing when to step down is a quality of an effective leader.

2
Temper Your Light or Lose It!

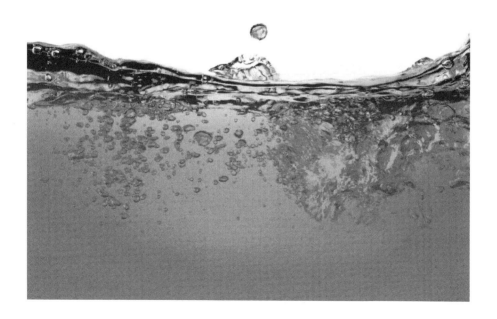

2
Temper Your Light or Lose It!

Dilemma

You were sitting in a training class and thinking about how you can move your career forward. The instructor called for a break and you begin to converse with a few participants. This particular training course included participants from both government and private sectors. It's kind of nice discussing the pros and cons of similar areas and of how both sectors while different, tend to have some of the same problems. While discussing your career aspirations with one participant, all of a sudden, he asked the question, "What do you want to be when you grow up?" You were stunned.

You're an educated professional with more than fifteen years experience in your field. It was a rather odd question, but was fair. Have you reached your full career potential? He goes on to tell you how your skills would really take you far in the private sector. You were working on the government side at that time.

The conversation did not cease after the training, but went on for weeks until finally, as they say in one of my favorite *Godfather* films; you receive an offer that you could not refuse. It was music to your ears to get an offer to work at one of the Big Four accounting firms. After all, your undergraduate degree is in Business and Administration with a major in accounting. Immediately after joining the firm, you really begin to fit in and enjoy the culture.

The first few weeks went well, but all of a sudden, those pesky politics began to creep into the workplace. It's not long before you find out whether you are really accepted into the firm or whether it was all a mirage. You find out who your competitors are and their aspirations at your level and above. Like everyone else, you want to do well at managing your team and handling the political environment. Your team has great ideas and performed well. The ideas are enterprising. It would have saved the company money; made the company money; given the company more recognition.

The honeymoon ended. One person was not buying what the team and you were selling. Would you believe that the one person who could have benefitted easily from the visibility and recognition that his team was enjoying who was not having any of it... your boss? Isn't it always the case that there is at least one person who waits to see how they can disrupt your plan? This was not the guy who brought you into the company but an aspiring senior manager who wanted to be recognized for partnership someday. You could not believe this was happening. You could have been contenders—the IT team to beat! This occurred for many reasons. Your boss and you had very different backgrounds— culturally and personality type. Your boss was introverted. Unfortunately insecure, he had a reputation for not working well with women. And, you are the complete opposite. You work well and talk with everyone. You embrace the differences to learn more about the cultures. You'd walk into the office expressing ideas and progress on the project, but the more you tried to move things along, the more your boss tried to control your progress. You enjoy communicating with everyone at any level in the company. These actions were viewed immediately as threatening. Shortly after joining the company, you were asked to meet with the partners and stayed late to work on proposals. You were really happy to be asked to work with other teams, even though your expertise was limited. They seemed to value your work effort and that made it worthwhile. You should have known that you were in trouble when, in the middle of a conversation with the team, one of the partners exclaimed, "Vickie will be moving into the partners' office next door." It was one of those moments when you wish that you had the skills of Samantha Stevens in the show "Bewitched" to wiggle your nose and disappear. You had just arrived at the new company and being partner hadn't even crossed your mind. Apparently, it was being discussed throughout the office. So in a subdued manner, you smile at the compliment and keep the conversation going without drawing interest from my other colleagues. The question in your mind was why would you want to move to an office that was smaller than a cubicle? It really wasn't like the office was a palace. It was small and you couldn't even fit a sofa in there. Yes, that and curtains are important items to have in an office.

Your boss overheard the remark and began distancing himself from you. All of a sudden, negative remarks about your work and team start to raise their ugly heads. It never dawned on you that he was secretly meeting with other partners and teammates regarding the office remark and somehow plotting your demise. You didn't know that your days were numbered. And then, out of the blue, one of the partners calls you in and utters the words no one longs to hear "... due to the limited budget... due to limited resources... due to whatever... we must let you go." You had no recourse but to pack your box and leave. The news spread through the office like wildfire but nothing was done. You had no recourse. You took it on the chin. Are you wondering what lessons you can learn?

Strategy

This was actually my story and the firing taught me a few valuable lessons in both leadership and politics that revolve around knowing your boss's management style and the cultural environment. Observe the lay of the land when you get a job. Determine who the players are and get a sense of the political culture so that you can manage the various management styles and avoid political minefields.

Is your boss outgoing or reserved? As an extrovert, for some, my personality could be over the top at times and could cause those who might not be ready for the outgoing type some sort of nerve damage. In fact, some introverts take viewing this as stressful and will try to avoid being around you. It's very easy for me to wake up with an extra dose of happiness and enter in a conversation on anything and everything. "Good Morning. How are you today? And on and on..." However, I have learned that happiness should sometimes be tempered depending on the personality type and environment. Don't try to change a person's personality to fit yours.

Advantage

Being fired taught me to welcome other personality types into the conversation. Manage upward and make sure that you make your bosses go from good to great. Even if circumstances center on your work efforts, always include your boss in the mix to show loyalty and respect. Don't outshine your boss because there are enough kudos to go around. In the end, you will be the one to soar like an eagle. Everyone will see you. You have not lived until you've been fired at least once and boy, it's a great character builder.

Reflection

Everyone has a bucket list of things you want to do before you leave this world. Much like the movie, the list can be really extravagant or not... it depends on where you are in your life. One thing for sure, the list can change over and over again. Interesting enough, some items will find their way onto the list without your knowledge. For me, that item was getting fired. You haven't quite made it until you have been fired. I can assure you that absolutely no one has that on their bucket list.

In my professional career, I have been fired twice. All it takes is one time, but when it occurs a second time, it gets your attention. Yes, it was painful, but there were so many political lessons to be learned. Have you ever been fired and didn't even see it coming? There I was going into the office each day. I had a great team who really cared about the mission of our company and our customers. I had wonderful work relationships with the senior management and co-workers. I participated in company events and was eager to volunteer for grass roots projects. Compliments were flowing like milk and honey. In all this bliss, one lingering problem was staring me in the face. Are you sharing the wealth with others or are you secretly stashing away coins for your own benefit?

Take-Aways

- Adjust to your boss's management style;
- Make sure your boss goes from good to great;
- Adjust to the cultural environment of your workplace;
- Observe the "Lay of the Land", those unspoken rules and expectations within your office. Don't suggest a dress-down Friday without considering your boss's Friday board meetings.

Vickie L. McCray

3
Dealing with Disappointments

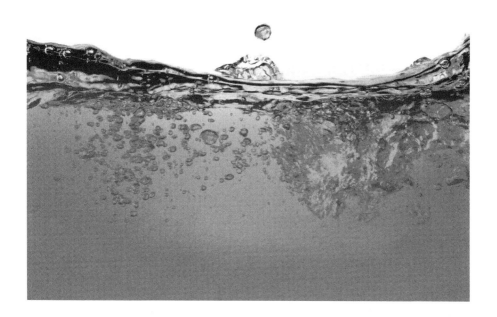

3

Dealing with Disappointments

Dilemma

Like getting fired, professionally, I have had a few ups and downs. Have you ever prepared for a job promotion and suddenly you find out that one of your best friends is in line for the promotion and gets the job? You didn't even know that they were interested in the job! What do you do when that happens? Well, I cried an entire weekend. After the waterfall ceased, I began to question why it occurred. Why? We are quick to question why any loss occurs. There's always a reason why anything occurs—good or bad.

There's a reason for everything and the reason is to show us that there is something bigger and better for us.

Strategy

What I have found is to believe that no matter what form of adversity is presented in your life, God has a greater plan for you. You won't see this plan right away. You've heard the saying, "When one door closes, another opens." The plan is bigger and better... It's there, stand still, believe it, and receive it. It's yours.

Advantage

Just so you know, I did not get a few promotions I thought I deserved. Had I gotten those promotions, my ego would have been the size of Lake Michigan. Also, I'd still be in Chicago.

Don't get me wrong, I love Chicago but my East Coast career has been instrumental in shaping me as a leader and in teaching the art of politics. There really was a plan for me. When adversity strikes, it's kind of hard to envision where you are and where you are going. Your sight and judgment are cloudy.

Reflection

Someone once told me that adversity is good for your soul. Adversity is a word that I have grown sto love. Everyone has had their fair share of adversity in their lives. I've compared it to a fine wine, a meal in Paris (Eiffel Tower of course), designer shoes (Stuart Weizmann), or designer clothes (St. John). Adversity is the best life has to offer to prepare you to overcome the ups and downs of life. Okay enough already... I love to day dream.

Got to admit, everyone likes to dress up and dine in one of their favorite hotels. Adversity is the best life can offer you to help you grow and become your best self.

In my life, adversity has come in other forms. It has come in the form of loss of family members and the loss of a promotion, to name a few. Like many of you, it can be devastating to lose family members. In my case, I lost both brothers in their twenties and thirties. As the eldest child, you have much responsibility to protect and nurture your siblings. You even fight to show authority and sometimes wish you were an only child. And when that happens, it is a very sad point in your life. My brothers and I were always a team. We talked all the time about nothing and had dance moves to die for. Even though we didn't have much money, we had love and that was enough.

It hasn't been easy living without them, but when I feel lonely, I reach back for a memory of my brothers to help me keep it moving to get me through those moments. That brings a smile to my face every time. I get by.

There is no way that I would have believed that I could go on with my life without my brothers. I talked with them all the time about everything. They were my support unit. I thought we would be together forever.

Take-Aways

1. Believe greater is coming;

2. When one door closes, another one opens.

Vickie L. McCray

4
Help, My Degree is Failing Me

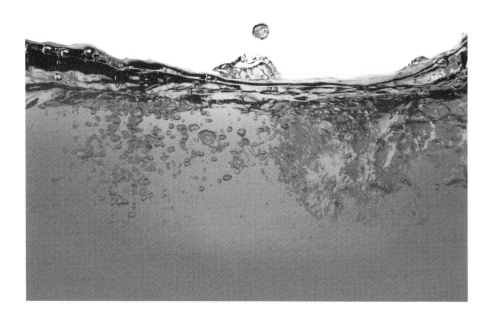

4
Help, My Degree is Failing Me

Dilemma

You receive your first assignment in your brand new job. You're a part of a team working on a project. It's as if you were back in college, but there's a new twist. Something doesn't feel right. Deadlines are being met, but something is missing. The team dynamics seem a bit off. One reason is the team wants to socialize and bond with each other.

What? You haven't got time for that! An occasional after---work drink at the pub or grabbing a bite to eat at the local eatery sounds good but... What would happen if you refused to go?

You're expecting to receive a pretty good rating since you went above and beyond the call of duty to get the job done. You worked long hours to research and analyze the areas of review. You conducted trend analyses and forecasted future results and profit margin. A yeoman's effort! Then the work performance review comes in. It's marginal. You let out a gasp, how could this be? Your mind begins to race with many thoughts of what you should do.

Strategy

Guess what? The effects could be felt in a number of ways, particularly at appraisal time. There are several options you could take.

Because you are mad as hell, the first thing you might want to do is request a meeting with your bosses to take another look at the rating and explain why you received something so ridiculous. After a cooling off period, you might want to reach out to human resources to get counseling on how to approach the issue. Should you file an Equal Employment Opportunity (EEO) complaint? Unless you can prove an egregious act performed by management and you have pictures, I would avoid this action at all costs. It's a career breaker. Another option, and one that I would vote for, would be to begin developing an improvement strategy to raise the rating for the next cycle. I would start being more of a team player. I would make sure that my work continues to be exemplary, including my team in the decision making process, and volunteer for difficult assignments. I would also make time to go out to lunch with the team, have a couple of drinks, and a bite to eat on occasion. It's not going to kill you. In fact, it might save you. In school, you often have to brush off your friends and social events to succeed. But at work, it is critical to bond with members of your team.

Advantage

You might not believe it, but these simple actions will change the team's opinion about your commitment to the project. It doesn't seem like much but it does work. Upon implementing this strategy, you may even become viewed as a "golden child"—someone who can't do anything wrong.

A valuable lesson is learned... one not taught in college: politics is present in everything you do, particularly in the workplace. The person who is successful in the workplace is not always the one that is highly educated, but the person who combines both knowledge and politics to get the job done. These tools are not taught in school but in your life lessons. Having a degree might get you in the game and may even keep you in the game but it's the combination of school smarts and street smarts, knowledge and politically suaveness that will catapult your career to places beyond what you could ever imagine!

Reflection

One of the crowning moments in life is when you receive your college degree. When I graduated from college there was this huge sigh of relief. My parents were overjoyed. It's time to go out into the world to apply all the things that you learned in four to six years. It was a fun time.

However, things suddenly change when you get your first real job. It's an eye opener. We all believe that when we go to college and graduate that we are ready to conqueror the world. In college, we worked long and hard to learn the basics. All that research, paper writing, and equation solving. The grades reflect commitment to the process and belief in the importance of a higher education. Nothing could be sweeter. But now I know college didn't prepare me for everything.

Take-Aways

- It takes school smarts AND street smarts, knowledge AND political suaveness to succeed in the workplace;
- In school, you often have to brush off your friends and social events to succeed.

But at work, it is critical to bond with members of your team;

- Socialize a bit... it won't kill you!
- Filing an EEO may hurt you and should only be done as a last option.

Vickie L. McCray

5
Foggy Expectations

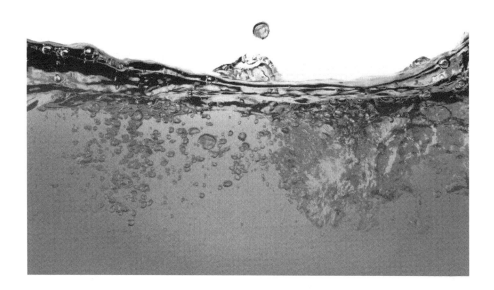

5
Foggy Expectations

Dilemma

They say no two snowflakes are alike. It's even truer in the professional world: no two supervisors are alike. Sometimes, when you perfect yourself for one boss, another one comes along and you have to re---perfect yourself again. That's what happened to me.

After being counseled by my supervisor, I was told that my writing skills needed work. What did I do? I hit the ground running, working daily on my writing skills. I searched out people in the organization who were renowned excellent writers. And one person stood out for me. We spent hours in the day writing reports and lunching on cabbage soup. Yes, we were also trying to lose weight. So much so, that after a few days we hated the smell of the soup! The best part of it all was my writing skills excelled. That was wonderful!

The not-so-good part of learning to write a certain way was that it would not be long before I was moved to work for another boss. Unfortunately, this boss did not focus on writing but on depth of knowledge. My new boss never defined his expectations of me. Previously, I was told that writing was important, and it is, but now there seemed to be a shift. Would someone give me a straight answer? It was confusing to say the least. In the time leading to the review, I received accolades and commendations. However, I received a poor review from my new boss. When I asked my new boss for clarification of the review, the words coming out of the boss's mouth just did not add up. How do you define and meet foggy expectations?

Strategy

As a program manager, I present the team with annual appraisals. Each team member has an opportunity to discuss their evaluations and provide feedback. They either agree or disagree. In each session, I make sure to say what I mean and mean what I say. I make sure the team understands their current roles, how well they are progressing, offer career advice, and develop a plan to assist the employee to receive a better rating for the next rating cycle. I make sure that what I say to the employee during the appraisal and the message they understood are the same.

That my word is true and the message would be the same even if I were approached ten years from now.

When wanting a clearer definition of their boss's expectations, employees can use these same elements. When starting with a new boss, ask how you'll be appraised (get documentation if available). Ask your boss for career advice and suggestions on getting a good rating.

Advantage

Keeping things straight is my mantra. Saying what I mean and meaning what I say builds credibility and trust. It is also a confidence builder for your team and for you.

Reflections

Have you ever worked for a boss that would say

something one week and change his or her mind based on another view that was voiced by someone else? There is a name for that type of boss: jellyfish. I've had a few jellyfish bosses in my career. They all have the same character traits, such as lacking credibility and untrustworthiness. With any boss, I try to anticipate what my rating will be. But on occasion, I was off base.

Take-Aways

- Create an environment of open communication;
- Clearly define your team member's roles and progress;
- Offer career advice to develop an improvement plan as needed;

- Be flexible and avoid thinking you've "learned it all" once you've improved your skills. Learning is a lifelong process.

6
Loyalty Balance, A Juggling Act

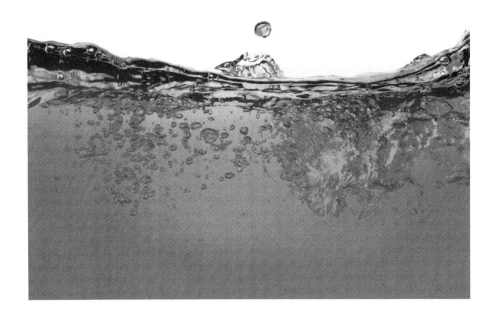

6
Loyalty Balance, A Juggling Act

Dilemma

I love to talk about certain traits and one of those traits is loyalty. As a manager, building team loyalty comes easily for me because I have found that to build loyalty, you must first build trust. The team has to know that you have its back, even when they might be wrong.

One of the team members made a mistake. The customer was not happy and expressed those feelings for a good amount of time. I knew that the team member had made a mistake. It was not intentional. The customer wanted to speak with the team member and me about the mistake. You know the type—they wanted to give me a piece of their mind. They wanted to show who was in charge. So, we listened and after hearing all this commentary, I said with a smile, "How are we going to fix it?" *We* being the operative word. What an incredible ice---breaker! The customer responded by smiling and working with us to face and overcome the challenge. I am not saying that this works in all cases, but the actions spread like wildfire throughout the team and office. The team recognizes that their leader is loyal, even when placed in uncomfortable situations.

How does one build loyalty? It starts by making yourself available to your team. It's not a bad idea to have an open---door policy. In some environments, this type of policy could mean trouble because team members may think of it as a way for disgruntled employees to tell on others. For me, having an open---door policy only means that you are never too busy to speak with your team about their concerns. Promoting the team spirit by keeping the team abreast of their performance and professional duties, conducting team meetings periodically to discuss the program and project matters, and holding appreciation luncheons to say "Thank you for all your hard work" to show the team how valuable they are to the project. Each day, make it a practice to walk around the office to say, "Good morning" to each team member. These actions could be misinterpreted as spying on the team members, but I want the team to know that I am in the office and available should they need me. These actions build loyalty and commitment among the team. These actions have shown the team that you have their backs. It's true... some team members will reciprocate, will look after you. But do they have your back? Do all these actions build loyalty? Well, now, that might just be a horse of a different color.

Strategy

I've learned that when it comes to loyalty, it might be a house divided. Loyalty is an individual measurement that can sometimes only be seen as far as your nose. I've learned that in spite of all these good deeds, loyalty will turn and run when opportunities present themselves. Sometimes, loyalty is based on "What can you do for me, now?" Yes, a few will actually be loyalists, but they are few and far between. Now that you know this, should you decide against taking care of others and forget about taking care of your team? Absolutely not!

Advantage

Leaders do the right thing even when no one is looking. They charge forward through public humiliation even if they have to stand alone and when others choose to go another way for personal gain.

Reflection

Like many leaders, I prefer loyalty. That is where I live. I consider myself a good soldier dedicated to the cause and mission. But you really can't blame anyone who chooses to leave your team when they are shown an opportunity that could lead to much greener pastures. So leaders continue to take care of those around them. You hope to instill the belief that when you look out for others, when you take care of others, at some point, the same thing will happen for you. It does happen and when it does, it sure is worth the wait.

Take-Aways

- Team-building strategies may or may not build loyalty;
- Sometimes loyalty is based on "What can you do for me, now?"
- You can't blame anyone who chooses to leave when they are shown an opportunity that could lead to much greener pastures;
- Continue to take care of those around you.

7
Win-Win

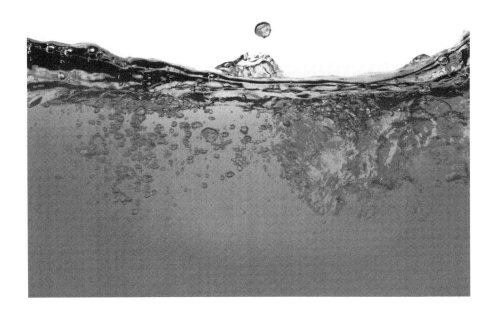

7
Leaders Choose Diplomacy to Achieve Win-Win

Dilemma

Every person in a management position and those selected for management positions believe that they are leaders. It never fails that when asked the question, "Do you consider yourself a leader?" they all respond resoundingly with an emphatic, "Yes!"

It's been my experience that one can be an effective manager without being a leader. However, it's really nice when you have good management skills and you are a leader.

The fundamental difference between the two is that managers manage and leaders lead with diplomacy. In leadership, I have learned that it's not so important to win the battle but to pick and choose those battles to win the war. Every disagreement is not the end of the world. It's important to evaluate each situation to determine a solution that will work for the betterment of your organization's mission.

You have been asked to prepare a strategic plan—one that will change the way you do business. You will have to get buy-in from all elements in the office—colleagues, co- workers, management...everyone. The problem that you face is while everyone agrees that change is good and needed, they don't believe that you are the person to lead the office to the promised land. Jumping into your own public relations campaign sounds like a good idea and could be effective, but could leave you tired and dismayed. Nevertheless, it's worth a try. This will be a huge undertaking.

The primary skill that I have used throughout my career is diplomacy. I practice using this skill daily. It is one that you can use anytime but not when you have a large project. The question that comes to mind is, "How do you eat an elephant... and the response is one bite at a time." Well in this case, the only way to tackle this elephant is in small bites. Managers and leaders need this skill to be successful.

So you develop a plan to deliver your strategy to the stakeholders. You carry out the plan in a variety of ways, including weekly brown---bag sessions or office---drive buys to visit those persons who might have questions with the whole process. You explain the pros and cons of the strategic plan, provide suggestions, and offer guidance for improvements. What happens next is worth its weight in gold. All of a sudden, you find that the barriers that were once quite prevalent are slowly coming down. Your public relations campaign is gaining in momentum in recognition because you are delivering the same message to everyone: "This plan is our plan for the betterment of the organization... and here is why and how you the team can make it successful." Many leaders use this approach to move an agenda forward effectively. It's when you choose diplomacy in actions to achieve a win-win outcome. It is not easy to have both but is worth a try.

Many people who really aren't leaders are placed

in leadership roles. You have to wonder how they got there. One reason may be due to the fact that there was an immediate need for a person to fill a team lead position. Unfortunately, when an unskilled team member is placed in a leadership position, mistakes start happening fast. The team dynamics are put to the test.

Throughout my career, I have seen this mistake happen over and over again. The team lead may or may not have leadership skills. It's not unusual for team leads to cater only to those individuals who possess the same skill sets. It's quite common for team leads to lack critical soft skills that would position them for leadership responsibilities. These soft skills might include rolling up your sleeve to help team members solve project problems, listening to team member suggestions, and even letting your guard down to empathize with a team member regarding a personal tragedy. We're only human.

Strategy

Effective leaders tend to have the ability to run projects/programs AND manage the team dynamics. This requires the ability to make sure that everyone knows that you understand their roles and to ensure that everything within the team dynamics runs smoothly. Some leaders believe you have to appear strong to be effective. I believe that striking a balance and giving stern direction with a smile is very effective. It works for me. A key is when giving direction, to make sure that your team understands the mission, the importance of their roles in completing the mission, and do a good job at selling the outcome—that it is for the benefit of us all. If you gain buy-in vertically and horizontally, it can be

easy to strike a balance.

Advantage

Your strategy as a leader can be successful in a leadership role if you choose a plan that is a win-win for the whole team and yourself. Striking a balance may sound easy, but it can be challenging.

Reflection

I have witnessed firsthand the tragedy of pretending you are a leader but you do not have soft skills. In this case, the leadership style comes off as dictatorial, insensitive, and often times, downright rude. In today's office environment, most teams are comprised of men and women. So, understanding the team dynamics is key to becoming an effective and efficient leader. Understanding the team dynamics also means understanding the politics of the team. You might have heard that men are from Mars and women are from Venus. Leadership and Politics are not the same, but they go hand and hand.

Take-Aways

- Effective leaders have the ability to run projects/programs AND manage the team dynamics;
- Giving stern direction with a smile is very effective;
- Leadership and politics are not the same, but they go hand and hand;
- Leaders use diplomacy to achieve a win-win.

8 Listening

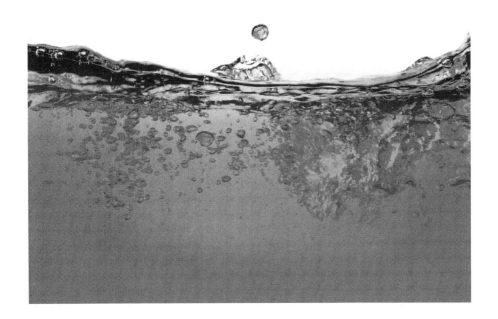

8
Listening:
Do You Hear What I Hear?

Dilemma

Throughout my career, I have been blessed to be surrounded by diversity, which is something I enjoy. The teams I have had an opportunity to manage have been diverse in ethnicity and skill sets. My teams are comprised of people who have PhDs to those who have GEDs. Ethnically, I've worked with Caucasians, African Americans, Africans, Koreans, Chinese, Vietnamese, Thai, Indians, and men and women from all these backgrounds. In this environment you learn who you are. It is also essential to understand the varying cultures and deliver the same message to everyone at the same time.

Communicating has to be done consistently and daily. An essential part of communicating effectively is listening attentively. My team is successful because their roles and responsibilities have been articulated to them and they understand what the mission and objectives are. People know whether you are listening to them or just going through the motions and nodding to whatever they are saying. The key is ensuring that the message being delivered is understood by everyone and is the same. Empower them to do their jobs the way they understand and be there to listen to them when they go off course. Guide teams to understand and manage and take risks when needed to come to a successful outcome. Leaders make sure that the message is understood by all and offer their listening ear to proceed forward to the goal. This is not always an easy thing to do. It has been a learning experience, but it does get better every day.

Strategy

You have to want it enough to get better at it. My one---on---one sessions and team meetings are quite entertaining. There is always good food and drink to create a calm and comfortable atmosphere. Everyone has something to say at the meeting, all members are respectful to one another, and the meetings never have major misunderstandings. Why is that? The leader has set the tone of the meeting. The leader has no expectations when communicating with the team. It is about the team.

Communication is conducted at whatever level

they are comfortable with. Listening is essential. Listening is not only by what you hear, but your body language. Believe it or not, your body cues speak louder than you know. They also send a message to the receiver of whether you are actually interested in the person and the conversation or could not care less.

Advantage

I tend to be very good at giving positive feedback during conversations. I share experiences and information and listen attentively. My extrovertness becomes invisible during the conversation. Communication and listening are great tools to have, especially when you're leading teams. Skills that have taught me to meet people where they are—no expectations, no fluff—just good ole conversation over coffee or breakfast! Before you know it, your office will become a revolving door.

Reflection

Do you think of yourself as a good communicator and listener? Or are you a good talker and a not so good listener? Not to worry, many people believe that they are great communicators and listeners. Believe or not, one of the critical attributes of effective communicators is that they are also very good listeners. As a leader and manager, this is a key skill to have.

Take-Aways

- Listening is a key component of effective communication;
- Communication is conducted at whatever level the team is comfortable with;
- Listening includes watching body language too.

Vickie L. McCray

9
Your Worst Fears

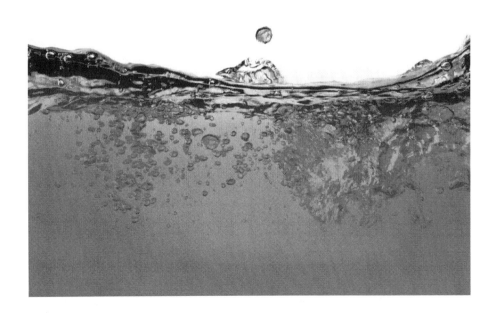

9
Your Worst Fears

Dilemma

I encountered other fears while attending middle school and college and even after obtaining my first job. Like many people, I faced fears that deci8ded to creep into my life: the fear of not being accepted by others, the fear of rejection, and the fear of hearing "no." These fears were present and were hard to take. I knew that I had to do something to overcome them. I needed to move past the fears to build my professional and personal careers. What did I do?

Strategy

I decided to face those fears straight on by asking the question, "What is the absolute worst thing that could happen if all those things occurred?" If you aren't accepted, if you get rejected, if you don't get promoted... what could happen? These challenges do not define you and you are not a failure.

Advantage

I've learned when things don't go the way I want, it only means that it is not the right time. I am reminded that your blessing might not come when you want it, but when it does come, it is right on time. In the meantime, while you are waiting, you have time to prepare yourself to overcome any challenges presented to you.

Vickie L. McCray

Reflection

As a child growing up in Chicago, I was active in church and loved to learn. It was never an option for me to miss going to church or attending school. These rules were instilled in my make-up. Another rule ingrained in my soul that I learned early in life was to listen to the teachings of the women in my family—my mom, my grandmother, and my aunts. I also learned that if I chose to go astray, there would be some furniture moving in my house... if you know what I mean. I feared this the most. I did not want to disappoint the family. So I worked hard to do the right thing to keep the peace. It would seem that the family and the village, the neighbors, were looking and keeping watch on my activities. I decided to turn the fears into challenges.

All of us have faced some fears, but it is how we decide to handle them. Take that fear and turn it into a challenge. You will be so proud of yourself. On the other hand, what if others do accept, you are not rejected, and the answer to the promotion you seek is "Yes". That can happen. The worse thing that could happen is that you SUCCEED! Your fear is turned into a challenge that could lead to massive success... the sweetest revenge.

Take-Aways

- Turn your fears into challenges;
- Move past the fears to enhance your professional and personal life;
- These challenges do not define you and you are not a failure.

10
Are You Ready for a Blessing?

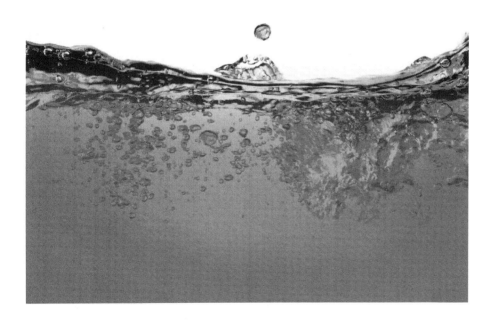

10
Are You Ready to Receive a Blessing?

Dilemma

Do you happen to know people who always want attention? It could be a sibling, best friend, or even a co-worker. They work feverishly to take the limelight from others even when they aren't in the light. No one is going to be better than them. Whether it is at work, church, family events, or out and about time, they just can't seem to shake hogging the microphone. These individuals always seem to make their rounds. They creep up and grab the attention just when no one is looking. The next thing you know, a special event, like a surprise appreciation award that was planned just for you, can quickly evolve into a '"Why didn't I receive an award?" discussion.'

Strategy

My leadership role continues to evolve into roles that include coordinator, team player, diplomat, and even advisor. It is important for me to let others shine. It is important to build confidence in others when necessary and be there to lead and guide without expecting anything in return. You've heard the rules: do unto others as you would have them do unto you. Teach a man to fish and he will never go hungry. Share the wealth and knowledge. Serve others.

Advantage

You may not believe this but when you make

giving an essential part of your life, the more you will be blessed. Share what you have because there is plenty to go around... and the windows of opportunities will open up to you. Get ready to receive your blessings!

While some may enjoy being the center of attention, I am the complete opposite. I tend to enjoy not being in the spotlight. It keeps me grounded. When others try to take the attention from me, I tend to let them have the spotlight. It is rather therapeutic for me to watch others if it is done in a manner that does not hurt anyone. However, where the attention is taken away to hurt the feelings of others, I tend to jump right in and offer down---to---earth solutions that are sometimes met with a little humor, to make the point that the actions are unacceptable.

My mom can revel in the spotlight. She is an outstanding gifted organist and gospel singer. She can really touch your soul with her organ skills and can raise the roof off the church when she sings a hymnal. I enjoy hearing and watching her in action. Folks often corner me and ask, "Can you sing like your mom?" My response begins with a smile, as I tell them, "No, I'm just happy to be in her company!" I'm so very proud of her, too! It makes me feel really good when folks recognize the good deeds of others and give flowers to those persons while they can smell and enjoy them. I love serving in runner-up positions. You know the ones that are not necessarily in charge but serve as deputy or assistant. The real mover and shaker positions. Public servants. These positions inspire camaraderie.

Yes, and in some instances, these positions promote competition. Who is afraid of a little friendly competition?

Take-Aways

- It is important to let others shine;
- Share what you have because there's plenty to go around;
- Don't block your blessings.

About the Author

Vickie L. McCray has more than twenty years of leadership and management experience in the United States Government (Agriculture and State Department) and private industry (KPMG, ManTech, Pragmatics, and E-9 Corporation). She has held positions as an audit manager, IT audit manager, technical advisor, project manager, and senior program manager.

Currently, she is the President and CEO of The McCray Group, Inc., a women/minority owned company specializes in providing executive leadership and oversight services to the federal government and private sector.

A strong believer in lifelong learning, McCray's educational background includes a B.S. in Accounting from Chicago State University and a

M.S. in Information Studies from Syracuse University. She also holds certifications as Certified Information Security Manager (CISM), Certified Government Financial Manager (CGFM), and Chief Information Officer (CIO), designated.

She and her husband Patrick McCray reside in Alexandria, VA.

Printed in France by Amazon
Brétigny-sur-Orge, FR